EIFFEL TOWER

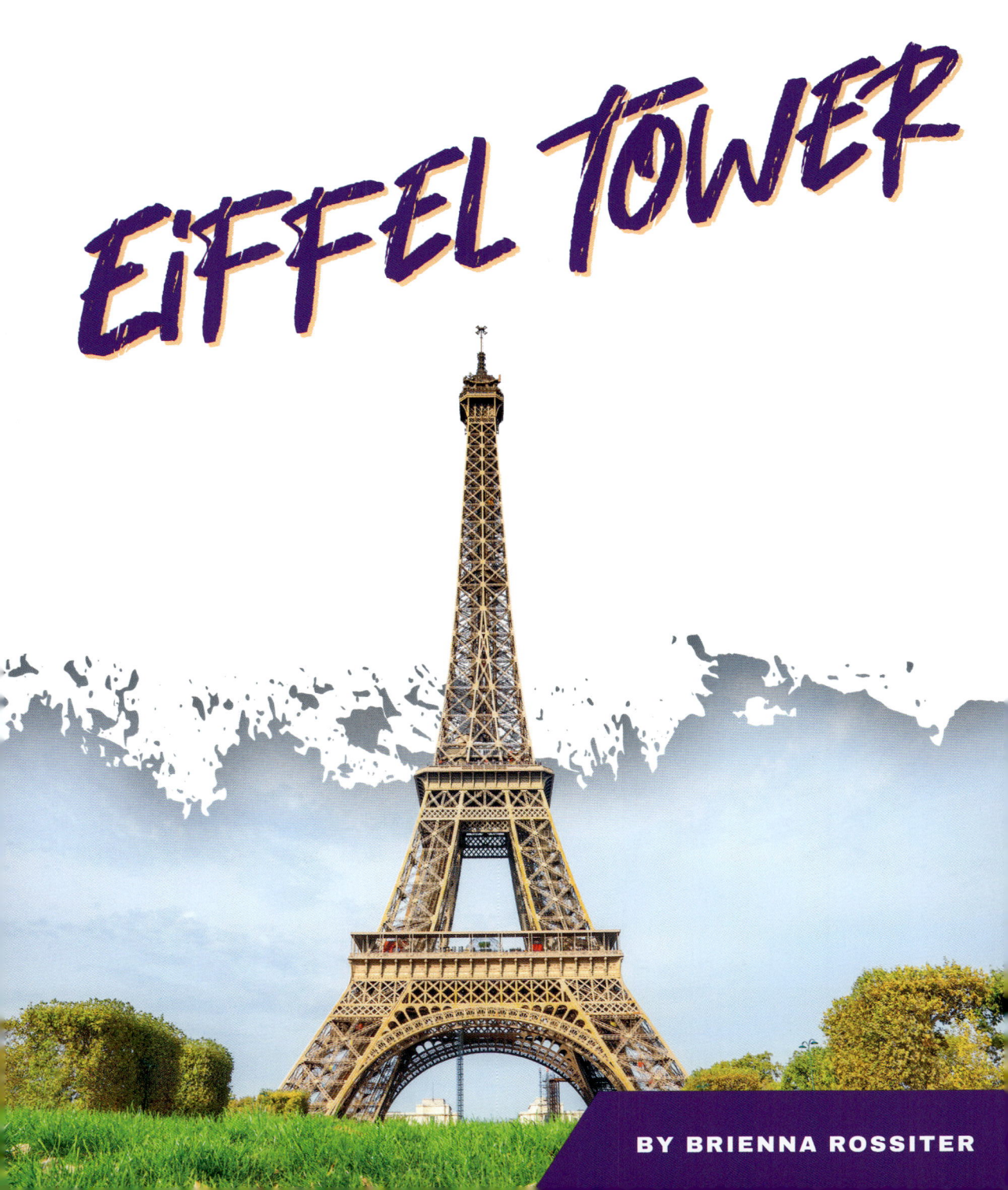

BY BRIENNA ROSSITER

Apex is distributed by North Star Editions:
sales@northstareditions.com | 888-417-0195

Produced for Apex by Red Line Editorial.

Photographs ©: Shutterstock Images, cover, 1, 4–5, 6, 8, 9, 14–15, 16–17, 22–23, 24, 26, 27, 29; Francois Mori/AP Images, 7; Musée Carnavalet, 10–11; Bettmann/Getty Images, 12; Wikimedia Commons, 13, 18–19, 20 (left), 20 (middle), 20 (right)

Library of Congress Control Number: 2023910664

ISBN
978-1-63738-748-1 (hardcover)
978-1-63738-791-7 (paperback)
978-1-63738-875-4 (ebook pdf)
978-1-63738-834-1 (hosted ebook)

Printed in the United States of America
Mankato, MN
012024

NOTE TO PARENTS AND EDUCATORS

Apex books are designed to build literacy skills in striving readers. Exciting, high-interest content attracts and holds readers' attention. The text is carefully leveled to allow students to achieve success quickly. Additional features, such as bolded glossary words for difficult terms, help build comprehension.

TABLE OF CONTENTS

CHAPTER 1

SYMBOL OF PARIS

The Eiffel Tower rises high above the city of Paris, France. The tower's base has four legs. These legs curve upward. They meet in the middle.

Paris is the largest city in France. It is also the capital.

Each leg of the Eiffel Tower is 82 feet (25 m) wide at the bottom.

Each leg is made of many metal **girders**. Girders also connect the legs together. They form three **horizontal** platforms.

LIGHT SHOW

The Eiffel Tower lights up at night. Golden lights shine from inside the tower. Each hour, lights flash. They make the tower sparkle for five minutes.

Each side of the Eiffel Tower has 5,000 light bulbs.

Elevators move up and down inside each leg. They carry people to and from the tower's platforms. There, people visit shops and restaurants. They also enjoy beautiful views.

The Eiffel Tower has seven elevators.

The tower's top platform is 906 feet (276 m) high.

CHAPTER 2

A NEW DESIGN

The Eiffel Tower was built for the World's Fair of 1889. France wanted to show off its greatness. So, it held a contest. Teams designed a tall tower for the fair's entrance.

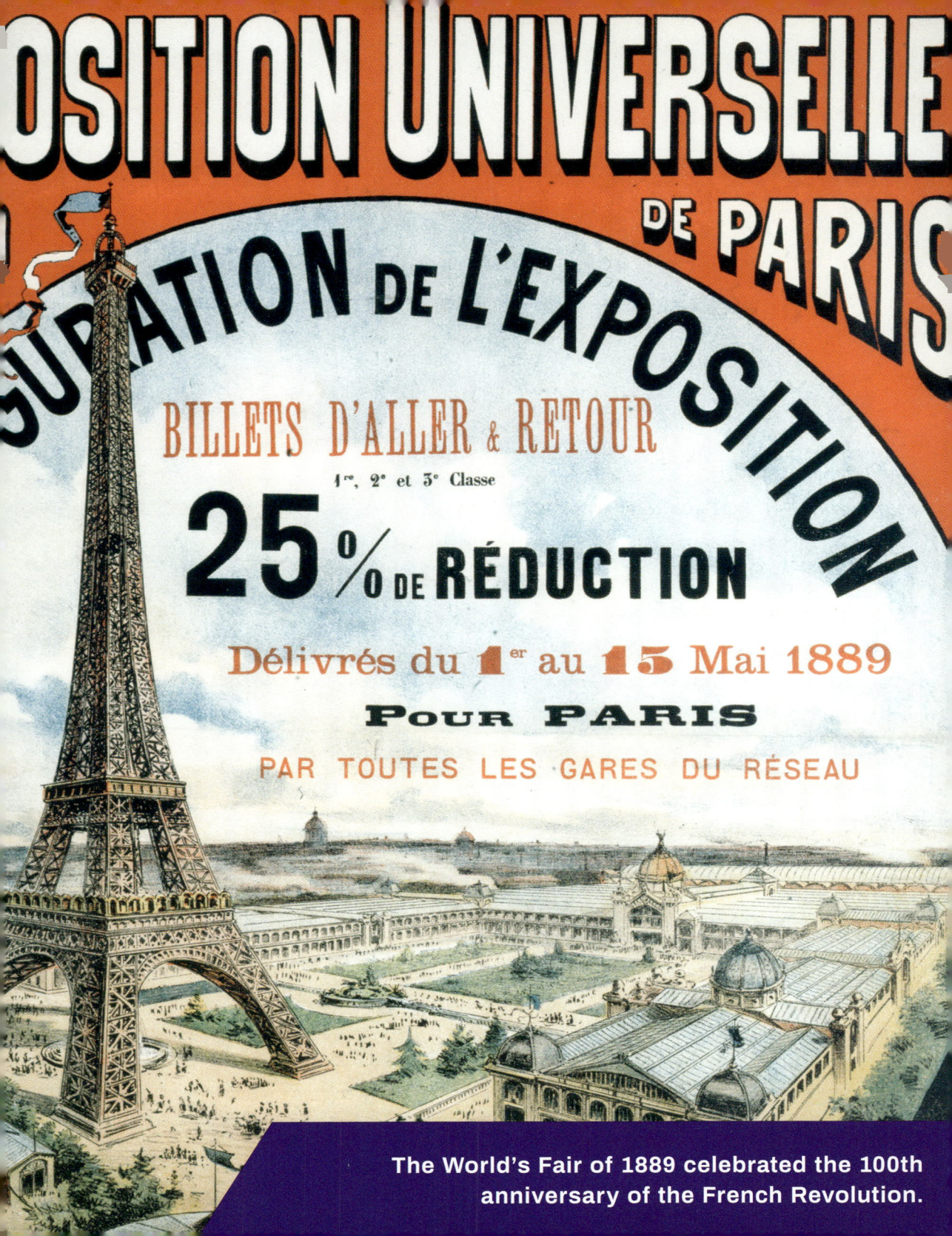

The World's Fair of 1889 celebrated the 100th anniversary of the French Revolution.

Gustave Eiffel's team won. At the time, many large buildings were made of stone. But Eiffel's team planned to use iron.

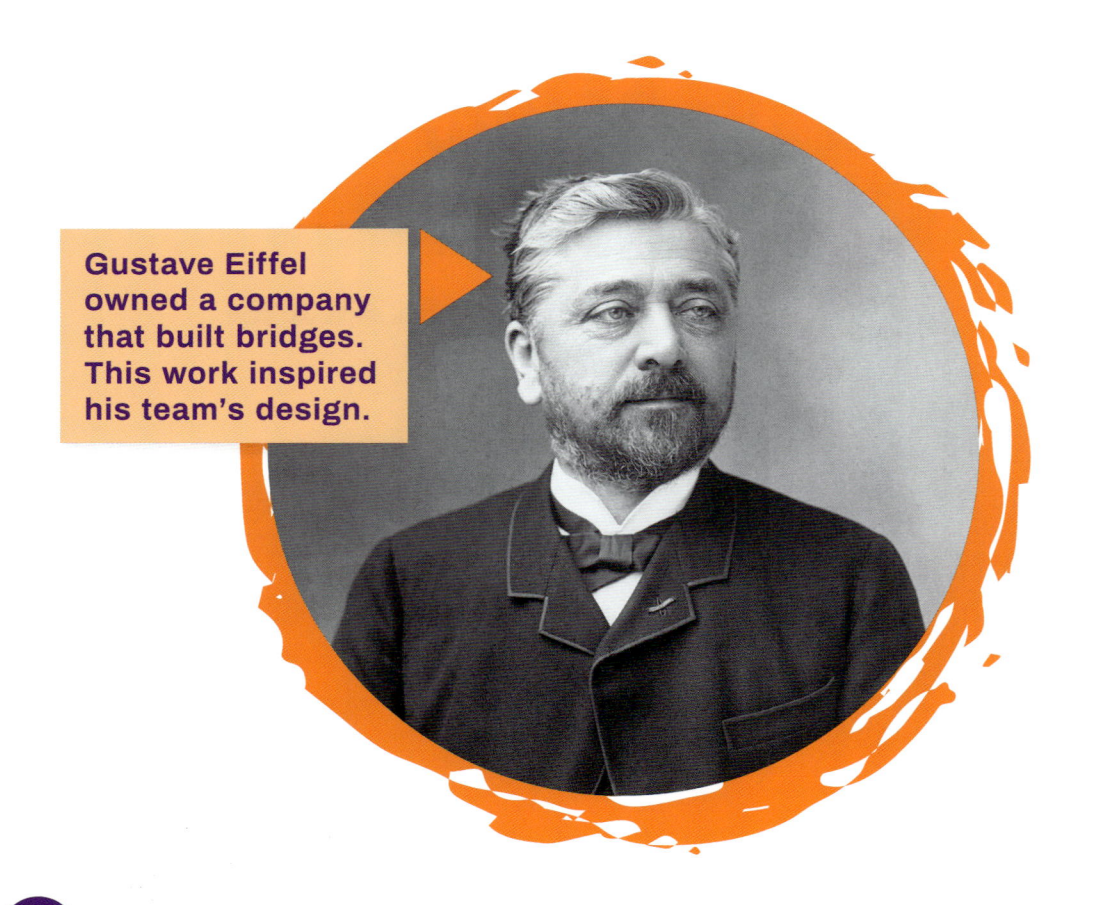

Gustave Eiffel owned a company that built bridges. This work inspired his team's design.

FAST FACT

Two **engineers** at Eiffel's company designed the tower. An **architect** helped them.

Eiffel also helped design the Statue of Liberty.

The Eiffel Tower's design let wind blow through the tower without causing damage.

Their tower would be made of crisscrossing girders. It would be huge but light. People had never seen anything like it.

RECORD SETTER

When finished, the Eiffel Tower stood 984 feet (300 m) tall. It was the tallest human-made structure in the world. It kept this record for more than 40 years.

CHAPTER 3

CONSTRUCTION

The Eiffel Tower was made with more than 18,000 metal pieces. Workers at a factory joined pieces together.

Each piece of the tower was made at a factory in Levallois-Perret, a few miles from Paris.

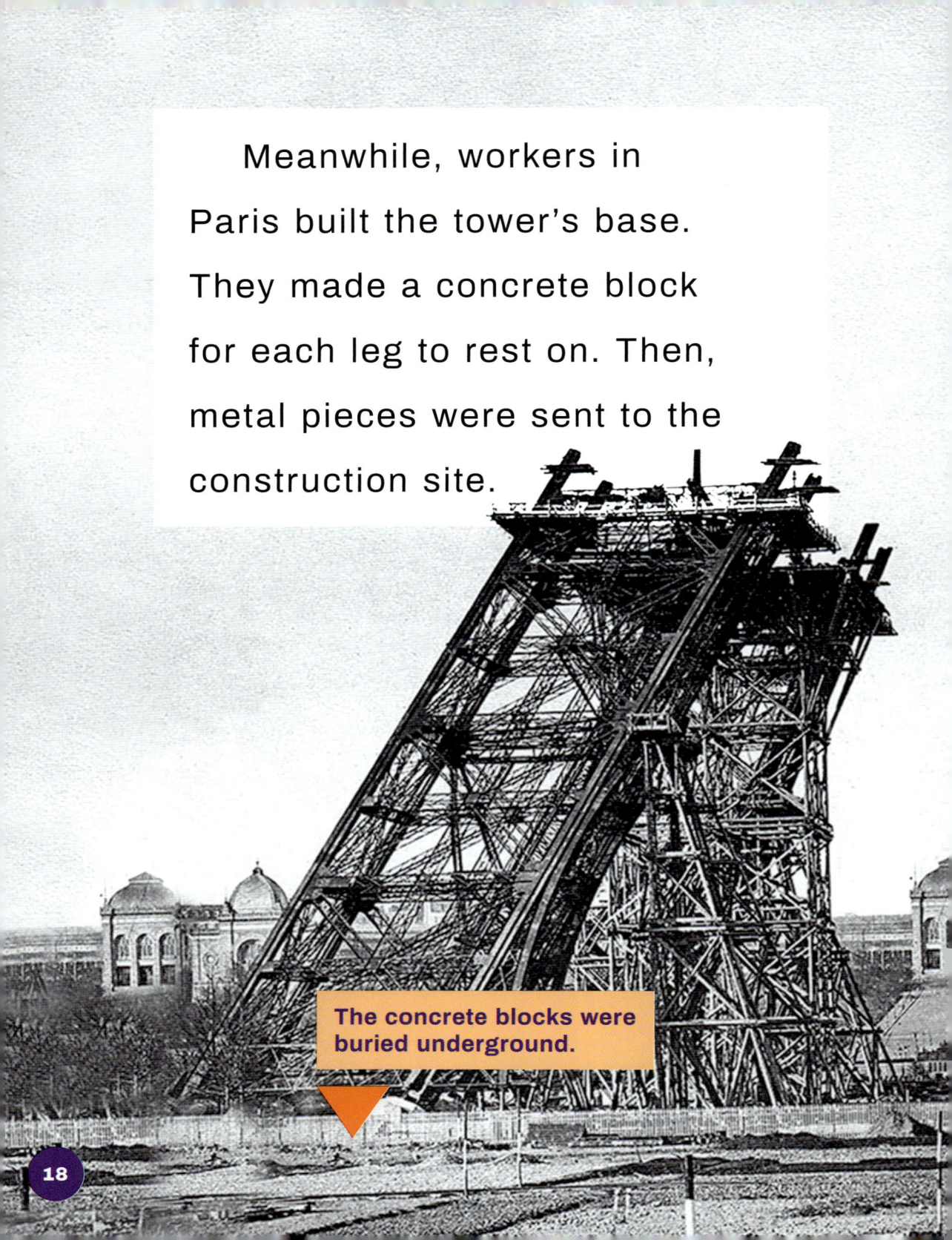

Meanwhile, workers in Paris built the tower's base. They made a concrete block for each leg to rest on. Then, metal pieces were sent to the construction site.

The concrete blocks were buried underground.

FAST FACT

Workers began digging in January 1887. Building work finished in March 1889.

Workers used **rivets** to link the pieces together. By May 1889, the tower was ready for people to visit.

REACHING HIGH

Wood **scaffolding** helped workers lift and place the metal pieces. Workers also used steam-powered cranes. The cranes slid up and down the tower's legs. Elevators later replaced the cranes.

Cranes pulled pieces up. Then workers placed them on parts of the tower that were already built.

CHAPTER 4

THROUGH THE YEARS

At first, the tower was only supposed to stand for 20 years. Then it would be taken apart. But it was kept because it proved useful.

The tower was originally supposed to be torn down in 1909.

Adding antennas made the tower even taller. By 2022, it reached nearly 1,083 feet (330 m).

People used the tower to do science experiments. It also held **antennas**. At first, they were only for radio. Later, TV antennas were added, too.

FAST FACT

Gustave Eiffel built a **laboratory** on the tower's third floor. He did experiments there.

Today, the Eiffel Tower is one of the world's most popular landmarks. Paint helps protect it from rust. People also watch for cracks. They hope to keep it safe for years to come.

The tower gets a new coat of paint every seven years. The paint helps block water and air, which can cause rust.

Millions of people visit the Eiffel Tower every year.

STRONG FEELINGS

At first, many people hated the tower's design. Some even signed a **petition** to stop it from being built. Most changed their minds later on.

COMPREHENSION QUESTIONS

Write your answers on a separate piece of paper.

1. Write a few sentences describing how the Eiffel Tower was built.

2. Would you want to go to the Eiffel Tower's top platform? Why or why not?

3. In what year was the Eiffel Tower finished?

    A. 1889

    B. 1909

    C. 2022

4. Why would people need to watch the tower for cracks?

    A. Cracks in the metal could weaken it.

    B. Cracks in the metal could cause less rust.

    C. Cracks could make the tower heavier.

5. What does **record** mean in this book?

*It was the tallest human-made structure in the world. It kept this **record** for more than 40 years.*

    A. a group of songs
    B. facts that are written down
    C. top height, length, or speed

6. What does **supposed** mean in this book?

*At first, the tower was only **supposed** to stand for 20 years. Then it would be taken apart.*

    A. meant
    B. questioned
    C. changed

Answer key on page 32.

29

GLOSSARY

antennas

Metal rods that send out or pick up signals for TV or radio.

architect

A person who makes plans for buildings.

engineers

People who use math and science to solve problems.

girders

Large metal beams used for building.

horizontal

Going from side to side, rather than up and down.

laboratory

A room or building where scientists do experiments.

petition

A formal request that many people sign and send to a leader.

rivets

Bolts that hold metal pieces together.

scaffolding

Layers of platforms around a large structure that let workers go up and down.

BOOKS

Smith, Emma Bland. *How Science Saved the Eiffel Tower.* North Mankato, MN: Capstone Publishing, 2022.

Spanier, Kristine. *Eiffel Tower.* Minneapolis: Jump!, 2021.

Twiddy, Robin. *A Visit to France.* Minneapolis: Bearport Publishing, 2023.

ONLINE RESOURCES

Visit **www.apexeditions.com** to find links and resources related to this title.

ABOUT THE AUTHOR

Brienna Rossiter is a writer and editor who lives in Minnesota.

INDEX

A

antennas, 25

B

base, 4, 18

E

Eiffel, Gustave, 12–13, 25
elevators, 8, 21
experiments, 25

F

France, 10

G

girders, 6, 15

I

iron, 12

L

legs, 4, 6, 8, 18, 21
lights, 7

P

Paris, France, 4, 18
pieces, 16, 18, 21
platforms, 6, 8–9

R

rivets, 21

W

workers, 16, 18–19, 21
World's Fair of 1889, 10

ANSWER KEY:
1. Answers will vary; 2. Answers will vary; 3. A; 4. A; 5. C; 6. A